Revedic Mathematics

Research in Vedic Mathematics

Volume - I

Dr. Dharmendra Kumar Yadav

Assistant Professor, University Department of Mathematics

Lalit Narayan Mithila University, Kameshwar Nagar

Darbhanga - 846008, Bihar

Notion Press

Dedicated to

Lovely Daughters

Palak and **Phalak**

and the Son Resting in Peace

Doman

Contents

Foreword

I read the manuscript and found that the book Revedic Mathematics is the short form of 'Research in Vedic Mathematics', which is a good initiative of writing the ancient mathematics knowledge in modern form. The author extended the works of the propounder of Vedic Mathematics Jagadguru Swami Sri Bharati Krishna Tirthaji Maharaja (March 14, 1884 –February 2, 1960).

This book is a result of a research article published by the author Dr. D. K. Yadav in 2007 with the title "Aanuruppen Binomial Method to Find the nth Power of Integers and Rational Numbers in Terminating Decimal Forms" in Acta Ciencia Indica, Mathematics, Vol. 33, Issue 2, Page No. 647 - 655.

Later the author with his co-author Mr. D. S. Knnojiya verified the method using C / C++ Computer software programming and found that the formulae run and give true results for all numbers.

Thereafter the author Dr. Yadav introduced it as a chapter with the title 'Anurupyena Binomial Method', which was published by Grin Verlag Publishing, Germany in 2018.

Revedic Mathematics contains the short cut methods to find the powers of any rational numbers in terminationg decimal forms, which is really a very fruitful book for the mathematics lovers. So I forward the book for the mathematics learners.

At last but not the least I would like to share that the author has guided a research scholar Mr. Rohit Ranjan Lal for his doctoral degree from University Department of Mathematics, Lalit Narayan Mithila University, Kameshwar Nagar, Darbhanga, Bihar on the topic entitled "Study of Vedic Mathematics Sutras in Context of Modern Mathematics and its Applications".

Therefore soon another book of the same title 'Revedic Mathematics: Research in Vedic Mathematics, Volume-II" will be available in the market and among the mathematics lovers with more extended formulae on Vedic Mathematics Sutras.

So I wish all the best to the author and the mathematics learners of this book.

Er. Nagendra Kumar Yadav

Director, Oracle Classes

Eksari Bigha, Sheikhpura, Bihar

24.09.2024

Preface

In this book a Vedic Mathematics Sub-sutra 'Anurupyena' has been analyzed and extended by the author Dr. D. K. Yadav to find the nth power of a number of any number of digits, of a rational number with terminating condition and of a decimal number by applying binomial theorem for positive integral index.

This is an attempt to correlate Vedic Mathematics Sutra with the Modern Mathematical concepts. Some students may find it difficult at first reading to understand the arithmetical operations but would play and enjoy it after some exercises.

The students studying in the lower class need not read the first two chapters and can directly go to the third chapter onwards. But if s(he) can understand the Binomial theorem and want to know the basic concepts of the Sutra of Vedic Mathematics, can read the first two chapters, although for finding the powers of a number of lower index like 2, 3, 4, 5, 6, etc., it is not necessary to look after it.

This is one of the reasons that the author has discussed the general working rule to find the nth power of a number in the last chapter. The book contains nine chapters and some excercises in each of the chapters. The learners are advised to do the excercises sincerely and also study the references given in the last of the book.

The research scholars pursuing or want to pursue for doctoral degree are advised to study the Vedic Mathematics book by Swami Sri Bharati Krishna Tirthaji first and then the research papers by the author for research oriented purpose, which are given in the references.

Thereafter they are advised to read the second book by the same author with his student Rohit Ranjan Lal entitled "Revedic Mathematics: Research in Vedic Mathematics, Volume-II" in future.

At last I wish the best wishes for the author Dr. Yadav for his great achievement of publishing this book.

Dr. Ayaz Ahmad

Head & Associate Professor

University Department of Mathematics

Lalit Narayan Mithila University, Darbhanga, Bihar

25.09.2024

Acknowledgment

The religious books have attracted me since my childhood. I have read many religious books like Mahabharata, Ramayana, Bible, Quran, Mahashivpuran, etc. I found that the religious books not only contains the stories of the almighty, if exists, but also the knowledge about the universe, that was propounded in the early stage of the civilization, when there was no science concepts available among the human beings. One such holy book is Vedas.

I have discussed about the Vedas in chapter one. As far as the working rules to find the different powers of a number is concerned, it has been developed and generalized by me in a series of three research papers Yadav (2007), Knnojiya & Yadav (2008) and Yadav (2018), which can be studied for details given in the references in the last of the book.

Although the first and third papers are almost same but the third one has been published as a chapter containing more examples than the first one, whereas the first one is a research paper, which was not properly written as per the latest format of research papers due to an independent researcher on the subject. That time in 2007, I was completely unknown about publishing a research paper, whereas the concepts of first paper was developed by me in 1997, when I was in B. Sc. Part-II Mathematics student.

The idea of a series of books on Research in Vedic Mathematics was in my mind since my graduation study time (1997) but I was waiting for my M. Sc. and higher degree with a job in an institution of teaching providing research facility, so that I can get some students of doctoral degree for research.

Now my one student of doctoral degree Rohit Ranjan Lal has completed his work on Vedic Mathematics Sutras entitled 'Study of Vedic Mathematics Sutras in Context of Modern Mathematics and its Applications' from University Department of Mathematics, Lalit Narayan Mithila University, Darbhanga and we have plan to publish that in a book with the same title as of this book. That's why it was named as "Revedic Mathematics: Research in Vedic Mathematics, Volume-I".

The present book will provide short cut formulae to find out different powers like 2, 3, 4, 5, 6, ..., etc. to n, of any number of any number of digits. So the learner will enjoy both the sutra and the short cut formulae discussed in the book.

Dr. D. K. Yadav

25.09.2024

Introduction

As far as the book is concerned, it is an extenstion book of the well known Vedic Mathematics Sutra propounded by Jagadguru Swami Sri Bharati Krishna Tirthaji Maharaj (1884 – 1960), who was Shankaracharya of the Goverdhan Math, Puri.

He studied Vedas and found sixteen sutras and thirteen sub-sutras based on Sanskrit Shlokas, which are very useful in studying many concepts of Modern Mathematics like Arithmetic, Algebra, Geometry, Calculus, Trigonometry, etc. The book Vedic Mathematics was first published in 1965 after the death of Swamiji in 1960. The work, Vedic Mathematics or 'Sixteen Simple Mathematical Formulae from the Vedas' was written by him during the period 1911 to 1918.

The author of this book Dr. D. K. Yadav has studied the book thoroughly and did many research work on it. He also successfully submitted a thesis on Vedic Mathematics Sutras with extension and analysis work with his research scholar.

I would like to recommend this Revedic Mathematics book to the learner and lovers of Mathematics. I with the author handover this book to the 20th century great Scientific Saint and Mathematician Jagadguru Swami Sri Bharati Krishna Tirthaji Maharaja morally, the writer and the propounder of the first published book on Vedic Mathematics.

After reading the book, it has been found that Swamiji compiled many mathematical concepts in only sixteen sutras and thirteen sub-sutras. After Srinivasa Ramanujan, I respected him a lot and treat him as a great mathematician of 20th century. His sutras are really too good to dominate the student's mind for many competitive examinations for short cut methods. So i dedicate this book to him first.

At last I thank Dr. Yadav to give me this opportunity to write few words about this book "Revedic Mathematics: Research in Vedic Mathematics, Volume-I".

Dr. S. N. Roy

Associate Professor

University Department of Mathematics

Lalit Narayan Mithila University, Darbhanga, Bihar

25.09.2024

1. Vedic Mathematics Sutras

The religious book Vedas are ancient Indian texts containing a record of human experience and knowledge. It is believed as the fountainhead and illimitable store-house of all knowledge. The *Vedas are Four* in number named as:

1. Yajur Veda
2. Sama Veda
3. Atharva Veda
4. Rig Veda

They have also *Four Upavedas*:

1. Ayurveda
2. Gandharvaveda
3. Dhanurveda
4. Sthapatyaveda

Mathematics is regarded to fall under the Upaveda of Artharvaveda called Sthapatyaveda. From this, Vedic Mathematics was rediscovered by **Swami Bharati Krishna Tirthaji Maharaja** (March 14, 1884 – February 2, 1960) of Govardhana Math, Puri during 1911 to 1918. After his death in 1960, the book Vedic Mathematics was published in 1965. His system of Vedic Mathematics is based on **Sixteen Sutras**:

1. Ekadhikena Purvena

2. Nikhilam Navatascaramam Dasatah

3. Urdhva-tiryagbhyam

4. Paravartya Yojayet

5. Sunyam Samayasamuccaye

6. Anurupye Sunyamanyat

7. Sankalana Vyavakalanabhyam

8. Puranapuranabhyam

9. Calana Kalanabhyam

10. Yavadunam

11. Vyastisamastih

12. Sesanyankena Caramena

13. Sopantyadvayamantyam

14. Ekanyunena Purvena

15. Gunitasamuccayah

16. Gunakasamuccayah

and **Thirteen Sub-sutras**:

1. Anurupyena

2. Sisyate Sesasamjnah

3. Adyamadyenantyamantyena

4. Kevalaih Saptakam Gunyat

5. Vestanam

6. Yavadunam Tavadunam

7. Yavadunam Tavadunikrtya Varganca Yojayet

8. Antyayordasake'pi

9. Antyayoreva

10. Samuccayagunitah

11. Lopanasthapanabhyam

12. Vilokanam

13. Gunitasamuccayah Samuccayagunitah;

These sutras describe the natural thinking pattern of mind. It is also a common belief that through Vedic Mathematics sutras, we use both part of our brain keeping us mentally fit. It deals mainly with various sutras and their applications for carrying out tedious and cumbersome arithmetical operations, and to a large extent, executing them mentally in short (Halai, 2018; Maharaja, 2015).

This is why the Vedic mathematics technique is rapidly emerging as a tool for various competitive examinations, where speed and accuracy play a vital role. It presents several very interesting methods to find the square and cube of any number in a few seconds. Unlike the traditional method, it is easy, interesting, and short (Maharaja, 2015). In this book, we will introduce the Vedic Anurupyena Sutra in finding the nth power of a number in different forms. But for this we need to know about the Binomial theorem for expansion for positive integral index, which has been discussed in the next chapter-2.

Exercise-1

1. Write the meaning of the sixteen sutras and thirteen sub-sutras of Vedic Mathematics.

2. Binomial Theorem

As far as the binomial theorem is concerned, Greek mathematician **Euclid** knew it for exponent 2, whereas the theorem for cubes was known in India by 6th century. The binomial theorem can also be found in the work of 11th century Persian mathematician **Al-Karaji**. The binomial expansion of small degrees was known in the 13th century mathematical works of **Yang Hui** and **Chu Shih-Chieh**. In 1544, **Michael Stifel** introduced the term "binomial coefficient", whereas **Issac Newton** is credited with the generalized binomial theorem for any rational exponent. It is stated as:

Binomial Theorem: We know that if a and b are two real numbers and n is a positive integer, then

$$(a + b)^n = C(n, 0)a^n + C(n, 1)a^{n-1}b + C(n, 2)a^{n-2}b^2 + \cdots$$
$$+ C(n, n - 1)ab^{n-1} + C(n, n)b^n$$

where

$$C(n, r) = {}^{n}C_{r} = \frac{n!}{(n-r)!r!} \text{ and } 0 \le r \le n.$$

Here n! is called 'factorial n or n factorial', which is defined as:

Factorial n: The product of first n natural numbers is denoted by n! and is defined as

$$n! = 1.2.3.4.5. \ldots (n-2).(n-1).n$$

For example, we have

$$1! = 1$$

$$2! = 1.2 = 2$$

$$3! = 1.2.3 = 6$$

$$4! = 1.2.3.4 = 24$$

$$5! = 1.2.3.4.5 = 120$$

$$6! = 1.2.3.4.5.6 = 720$$

Putting different values of n in the Binomial theorem, we can find the following formulae, which will be used in the book later. So putting n = 1, 2, 3, 4, 5, 6 in the above theorem, we get

$$(a+b)^1 = a+b$$

$$(a+b)^2 = a^2 + 2ab + b^2$$

$$(a+b)^3 = a^3 + 3a^2b + 3ab^2 + b^3$$

$$(a+b)^4 = a^4 + 4a^3b + 6a^2b^2 + 4ab^3 + b^4$$

$$(a+b)^5 = a^5 + 5a^4b + 10a^3b^2 + 10a^2b^3 + 5ab^4 + b^5$$

$$(a+b)^6 = a^6 + 6a^5b + 15a^4b^2 + 20a^3b^3 + 15a^2b^4 + 6ab^5 + b^6$$

If we know to find the values of factorial n and of C(n, r), we can find the expansion of (a + b) for any value of n from Binomial theorem. For the students studying in lower classes, we can use the Pascal's triangle to find the values of C(n, r) in the expansion of the Binomial theorem as follows:

Pascal's Triangle

Value of n															
								Coefficients in Binomial Expansion							
0								1							
1							1		1						
2						1		2		1					
3					1		3		3		1				
4				1		4		6		4		1			
5			1		5		10		10		5		1		
6		1		6		15		20		15		6		1	
7	1		7		21		35		35		21		7		1

We can observe the coefficients in the earlier expansion for different powers and match the coefficients from this table. Making such a table for higher values of n, we can write the Binomial expansion for any positive integral n.

Exercise-2

1. Find the values of factotial n for n = 7, 8, 9, 10, 12, 15, 18.
2. Make the Pascal's triangle for n = 12, 15, 18, 20.
3. Write the Binomial expansion of $(a + b)^n$ for n = 7, 8, 9, 10.

3. Anurupyena Sutra

Swamiji states that the upasutra or sub-formula or sub-sutra '*Anurupyena*' means 'proportionately'. In actual application, it connotes that, in all cases where there is a rational ratio-wise relationship, the ratio should be taken into account and should lead to a proportionate multiplication or division as the case may be.

In other words, when neither the multiplicand nor the multiplier is sufficiently near a convenient power of 10 which can suitably serve as a base, we can take a convenient multiple or sub-multiple of a suitable base, as our 'working base', perform the necessary operation with its aid and then multiply or divide the result proportionately, i.e. in the same proportion as the original base may bear to the working base actually used by us. This is used in multiplying two numbers and so useful in finding square, cubes, etc.

Sharma et al. (2024) states that this sub-formula is used to find the square of a number, which is neither near to base number nor near to sub-base number, for example 66. **Shashtri** (2011) states the limits of this upasutra that this is useful for all those numbers which are of two or three digits numbers.

The meaning of "Anurupyena" is "proportionately". This is an upasutra of Ekadhikena Purvena sutra (Maharaja, 2015; Shashtri, 2011). Anurupyena Vedic Sutra is based on the concept of geometric progression (Thakur, 2019).

This method is best suited for cubing a small number comfortably. Though we can find the cube of a bigger number using this method, but that will involve more calculations (Shashtri, 2011; Thakur, 2019).

As far as the concept of geometric progression is concerned in its application in the sutra, we can observe its presence in the formula for finding the cube of a positive number. For it we divide the given number 'ab' into two parts a and b from left and right side respectively, where a and b can have any number of digits, i.e. ab is a number of any number of digits and it is not a multiplication of a and b. The working rule to find the cube is as follows:

i. First take the cube of the first part 'a'.

ii. Multiply a with the common ratio $\frac{b}{a}$, in a row for three more terms to find $a^3, a^3.\frac{b}{a}, a^3.\frac{b^2}{a^2}, a^3.\frac{b^3}{a^3}$.

iii. Double the second and third terms and put them down below the second and third terms.

iv. Finally add the two rows,

like below in table-1:

	First Term	Second Term	Third Term	Fourth Term
$(ab)^3$	a^3	$a^3 \cdot \dfrac{b}{a}$ $= a^2 . b$	$a^3 \cdot \dfrac{b^2}{a^2}$ $= a . b^2$	$a^3 \cdot \dfrac{b^3}{a^3}$ $= b^3$
Double M.T.		$2 . a^2 . b$	$2 . a . b^2$	
Add	a^3	$3 . a^2 . b$	$3 . a . b^2$	b^3

M.T. means middle terms.

Shashtri (2011) states this sutra for two digits number 'ab' as:

$$(ab)^3 = a^3 \mid 3 . a^2 . b \mid 3 . a . b^2 \mid b^3$$

and for three digits number 'abc' as:

$$(abc)^3 = (ab)^3 \mid 3 . (ab)^2 . c \mid 3 . (ab) . c^2 \mid c^3$$

Then the required number of digits is taken from right most side from each term and the remaining number is then added to its left side. Let us consider some examples as:

Example-1: Find the cube of 13.

Solution: Here, a = 1, b = 3, and $\frac{b}{a} = \frac{3}{1} = 3$. Hence the arrangement of four terms will be as

$$(13)^3 = 1 \mid 9 \mid 27 \mid 27$$

Taking one digit from right side and adding the remaining digits to its left, we get

$$= 1\,|\,9\,|\,27\,|\,27 = 1\,|\,9\,|\,27+2\,|\,7 = 1\,|\,9\,|\,29\,|\,7$$
$$= 1\,|\,9+2\,|\,9\,|\,7$$

$$= 1\,|\,11\,|\,9\,|\,7 = 1+1\,|\,1\,|\,9\,|\,7 = 2\,|\,1\,|\,9\,|\,7 = 2197$$

Example-2: Find the cube of 103.

Solution: Here taking a = 10 and b = 3, we get the arrangement of four terms as

$$(103)^3 = 1000\,|\,900\,|\,270\,|\,27$$

Taking one digit from right side and adding the remaining digits to its left, we get

$$= 1000\,|\,900\,|\,272\,|\,7 = 1000\,|\,927\,|\,2\,|\,7 = 1092\,|\,7\,|\,2\,|\,7$$

$$= 1092727$$

But in the text books and research papers, no statement is found that 'how many digits should we take?, if we have to find the cube of a r-digit number using this sutra. Let us analysis the working procedures and try to find the pattern, it follows.

We have discussed the formulae to find the cube of a number in the previous section as: for two digit numbers 'ab', it is

$$(ab)^3 = a^3\,|\,3.a^2.b\,|\,3.a.b^2\,|\,b^3$$

and for three digits number 'abc' it is:

$$(abc)^3 = (ab)^3 \mid 3.(ab)^2.c \mid 3.(ab).c^2 \mid c^3$$

If we express the number in decimal representation and expand it using Binomial theorem for positive integral index, we get

$$(10a + b)^3 = (10a)^3 + 3.(10a)^2.b + 3.(10a).b^2 + b^3$$

$$= 1000.a^3 + 300.a^2.b + 30.a.b^2 + b^3 \qquad (1)$$

Here after adding the first three terms the resultant will have at least one zero at unit place, so the unit digit number of fourth term b^3 will be written directly to write the cube of the given number. Obviously the digit at tenth place in the fourth term will be added to the digit at the tenth place in the third term, because the digit at the tenth places in first and second term will be zero. Similarly the digit at the hundredth place in third term will be added to the digit at the hundredth term in the second term as the digit at the hundredth term in the first term is zero. The digit at thousandth place in the second term will be added with the non-zero digit of the first term at thousandth place and onwards towards its left side and so on for other digits. Similar logic will be implemented for three digit numbers having zero in its middle, like 'a0b' as a number, as

$$(100a + b)^3 = (100a)^3 + 3.(100a)^2.b + 3.(100a).b^2 + b^3$$

$$= 1000000.a^3 + 30000.a^2.b + 300.a.b^2 + b^3$$

But if the middle term in three digit number is not zero, then since we divide the number in two parts as 'ab' and 'c', the previous logic will be implemented on 'ab' separately to find its square and cube to put these values in the above formula. Thus the logic discussed above is hidden in the short-cut formula of Vedic Anuruppyena sutra.

We clearly see the pattern of the procedures in the above examples and analysis. Based on these patterns, **Yadav** (2007) has propounded Anurupyena Binomial Method to find the nth power of any integer of any number of digits and a rational number with terminating condition. He observed certain special pattern of calculation in finding the square and cube of integers using Vedic sutra but some limitations have also been found in the application of this sutra. No general rule has been mentioned in the Vedic Mathematics text books or in any others to find the nth power of any integers. He combined the Anurupyena sutra and Binomial theorem for positive integral index to result out the method. That's why it has been named as **Anurupyena Binomial Method**. Before going to the general method of finding the powers of any numbers, let us start from the square, cube, etc. and then increasing the powers values, we in last, will discuss the general method.

Exercise-3

1. Write some applications of the Anurupyena sub-sutra.
2. Discuss the meaning of Anurupyena sutra and explain it.

4. Square of a Number

To find the square of any positive integer of any number of digits, we break the given number into two parts A starting from the left hand side digit and B the remaining digits of the given number from right side, using the process discussed in last chapter. If the given number has even number of digits, both A abd B have equal number of digits. But if the number of digits is odd, then A has one more digit than B. This rule is also true for all cases discussed in next chapters (Maharaja, 2015; Yadav, 2007, 2008, 2018). Thereafter we proceed as follows:

1. We make 3 columns and write the three terms of right hand side of the binomial theorem for positive integral index

$$(A+B)^2 = {}^2C_0 A^2 + {}^2C_1 A^1 B^1 + {}^2C_2 B^2$$

as follows:

$$\begin{array}{ccc} Column-1 & Column-2 & Column-3 \\ A^2 & 2 \times A \times B & B^2 \end{array}$$

2. Evaluate each column separately.
3. Divide the number of digits (R) of the given number by 2 and find the quotient Q. Q may be found as: If R=2m + 1 or 2m, where m is a positive integer, then Q = m.

4. Now to find the required result we combine all 3 parts as follows:

i. Take as many digits as the quotient value is from the right hand side of column-3 (let it be P_3) and add the remaining digits (number) in its left hand side in column–2.

ii. Again take as many digits as the quotient value is from the right hand side of the column–2 (let it be P_2) and write it in the left side of P_3 (like P_2 P_3) and add the remaining digits (number) in its left hand side in column-1.

iii. Finally find the number P_1 in column-1 after adding remaining digits (numbers) of column–2 and write P_1 to the left of P_2.

Thus we find the square of the positive integer as $P_1P_2P_3$.

Let us explore the method with following examples:

Example 1: Find the square of 13.

The given number is of 2 digit, therefore R = 2, A = 1, B = 3. We make the three columns as:

$$Column-1 \quad Column-2 \quad Column-3$$
$$A^2 \qquad\quad 2AB \qquad\quad B^2$$
$$1^2 = 1 \qquad 2\times1\times3 = 6 \qquad 3^2 = 9$$

Thus $13^2 = 169$. Since here R = 2, Q = 1, we take only one digit from right hand side of column-3 & column-2 respectively.

Example 2: Find the square of 312.

Here R = 3, A = 31, B = 2. We make the three columns as:

$$
\begin{array}{ccc}
Column-1 & Column-2 & Column-3 \\
A^2 & 2AB & B^2 \\
31^2 = 961 & 2\times 31\times 2 = \underline{12}4 & 2^2 = 4 \\
\underline{+12} & 4 & 4 \\
973 & 4 & 4
\end{array}
$$

Thus $31^2 = 97344$. Here R = 3, Q = 1, therefore we have taken one digit from right hand side. The underlined number in column-2 has been added in its left side in column-1.

Example 3: Find the square of 8394.

Here R = 4, A = 83, B = 94. We make the three columns as:

$$
\begin{array}{ccc}
Column-1 & Column-2 & Column-3 \\
A^2 & 2AB & B^2 \\
83^2 = 6889 & 2\times 83\times 94 = 15604 & 94^2 = \underline{88}36 \\
\underline{+156} & \underline{+88} & 36 \\
7045 & \underline{15692} & 36
\end{array}
$$

Thus $8394^2 = 70459236$. Here R = 4 and Q = 2. Therefore we have taken two digits from right hand side.

Example 4: Find the square of 33333.

Here R = 5, A = 333, B = 33. We make the three columns as:

Column -1	Column -2	Column -3
A^2	$2AB$	B^2
$333^2 = 110889$	$2 \times 333 \times 33 = 21978$	$33^2 = \underline{10}89$
$\underline{+219}$	$+10$	89
111108	$\underline{21988}$	89

Thus $33333^2 = 1111088889$. Here R = 5 and Q = 2, Therefore we have taken two digits from right side.

Example 5: Find the square of 389456.

Here R = 6, A = 389, B = 456. We make the three columns as:

Column -1	Column -2	Column -3
A^2	$2AB$	B^2
$389^2 = 151321$	$2 \times 389 \times 456 = 354768$	$456^2 = \underline{207}936$
$\underline{+354}$	$+207$	936
151675	$\underline{354}975$	936

Thus $389456^2 = 151675975936$. Here R = 6 and Q = 3, Therefore we have taken three digits from right hand side.

Example 6: Find the square of 1111111111.

Here R = 10, A = 11111, B = 11111. We make the three columns:

Column-1	Column-2	Column-3
A^2	2.A.B.	B^2
$11111^2 = 123454321$	246908642	$11111^2 = 123454321$

+2469	+1234	54321
=123456790	=246909876	
123456790	09876	54321

Thus $11111111111^2 = 12345679000987654321$. Here R = 10 and Q = 5, therefore we have taken five digits from right side.

Example 7: Find the square of 1000.

Here R = 4, A = 10, B = 00. We make the three columns as:

$$\begin{array}{ccc} Column-1 & Column-2 & Column-3 \\ A^2 & 2AB & B^2 \\ 10^2 = 100 & 2 \times 10 \times 00 = 0 & 00^2 = 0 \\ 100 & 00 & 00 \end{array}$$

Thus $(1000)^2 = 1000000$. Here R = 4 and Q = 2, therefore we have taken two digits from right side of column-3 and column-2 respectively. Since we have to take two digits from the right side of column-3 and column-2, therefore we can write 0 = 00.

Example 8: Find the square of 6.

Here the given number is of only one digit and to apply the method, we must have at least two digits. Therefore we write it as 6 = 06. Now R = 1, A = 0, B = 6. We make the three columns as:

$$\begin{array}{ccc} Column-1 & Column-2 & Column-3 \\ A^2 & 2AB & B^2 \\ 0^2 = 0 & 2 \times 0 \times 6 = 0 & 6^2 = \underline{3}6 \\ 0 & +3 & 6 \\ 0 & 3 & 6 \end{array}$$

Thus $(6)^2 = (06)^2 = 36$. Here A = 0 and Q = 1, therefore we have taken one digit from the right hand side of column-3 and column-2 respectively.

Exercise-4

1. Find the square of the numbers 85, 98, 76, 36, 79.

2. Find the square of the numbers 343, 567, 987, 458.

3. Find the square of the numbers 453497546, 9746486.

4. Can we make some another rule to find the square of any positive number?

5. Can we extend this method for negative numbers also?

6. Can we apply the working rules for a fraction also?

7. Can we find the square of an irrational number using the above method?

Hints: The answers of the last three questions will be available for the readers after reading the complete book. They have been discussed in the ninth chapter.

5. Cube of a Number

To find the third power or cube of any positive integer of any number of digits, we break the given number into two parts A starting from the left side digit and B the remaining digits of the given number using the process discussed earlier in chapter-4 (Yadav, 2007, 2008, 2018). Thereafter we proceed as follows:

1. Make 4 columns and write the 4 terms of right hand side of the binomial theorem for positive integral index

$$(A + B)^3 = {}^3C_0 A^3 + {}^3C_1 A^2 B^1 + {}^3C_2 A^1 B^2 + {}^3C_3 B^3$$

    as follows:

$Column-1$	$Column-2$	$Column-3$	$Column-4$
A^3	$3 \times A^2 \times B$	$3 \times A \times B^2$	B^3

2. Evaluate each column separately.
3. Divide the number of digits R of the given number by 2 and find the quotient Q. Q may also be found as: If R = 2m+1 or 2m, where m is a positive integer, then Q = m.
4. Now to find the required result we combine all 4 parts as:

i.   Take as many digits as the quotient value is from the right side of column-4 (let it be P_4) and add the remaining digits (number) in its left side in column–3.

ii. Again take as many digits as the quotient value is from the right side of the column–3 (let it be P_3) and write it in the left side of P_4 (like P_3 P_4) and add the remaining digits (number) in its left side in column-2.

iii. Repeat (i) and (ii) up to column-2 till P_2 and finally find the number P_1 in column-1 after adding remaining digits (numbers) of column–2 and write P_1 to the left of P_2.

Thus we find the required 3rd power of the given positive integer as $P_1P_2P_3P_4$.

Let us see the method working in finding the cube of the numbers as:

Example 1: Find the cube of 68.

Here the given number is of two digits, therefore R=2, A=6, B=8. Now we make the four columns as follows:

$Column-1$	$Column-2$	$Column-3$	$Column-4$
A^3	$3 \times A^2 \times B$	$3 \times A \times B^2$	B^3
$6^3 = 216$	$3 \times 6^2 \times 8 = 864$	$3 \times 6 \times 8^2 = 1152$	$8^3 = \underline{512}$
$+98$	$+120$	$+51$	2
314	$\underline{984}$	$\underline{1203}$	2

Thus $68^3 = 314432$. Here R=2, Q=1. Therefore we have taken one digit from right side of column-4, column-3, and column-2 respectively.

Example 2: Find the cube of 668.

Here the given number is of three digits, therefore R = 3, A = 66, B = 8. Now we make the four columns as follows:

$Column-1$	$Column-2$	$Column-3$	$Column-4$
A^3	$3\times A^2 \times B$	$3\times A\times B^2$	B^3
$66^3 = 287496$	$3\times 66^2 \times 8 = 104544$	$3\times 66\times 8^2 = 12672$	$8^3 = \underline{5}12$
$+10581$	$+1272$	$+51$	2
298077	$\underline{105816}$	$\underline{12723}$	2

Thus $668^3 = 298077632$. Here R = 3 and Q=1, therefore we have taken one digit from right side.

Example 3: Find the cube of 3333.

Here the given number is of four digits, therefore R = 4, A = 33, B = 33. Now we make the four columns as follows:

$Column-1$	$Column-2$	$Column-3$	$Column-4$
A^3	$3\times A^2 \times B$	$3\times A\times B^2$	B^3
$33^3 = 35937$	$3\times 33^2 \times 33 = 107811$	$3\times 33\times 33^2 = 107811$	$33^3 = \underline{35}937$
$+1088$	$+1081$	$+359$	37
37025	$\underline{108892}$	$\underline{108170}$	37

Thus $3333^3 = 37025927037$. Here R=4 and Q=2, therefore we have taken two digits from right side.

Example 4: Find the cube of 1000.

Here the given number is of four digits, therefore R = 4, A = 10, B = 00. Now we make the four columns as follows:

$Column-1$	$Column-2$	$Column-3$	$Column-4$
A^3	$3 \times A^2 \times B$	$3 \times A \times B^2$	B^3
$10^3 = 1000$	$3 \times 10^2 \times 00 = 0$	$3 \times 10 \times 00^2 = 0$	$00^3 = 0$
1000	0	0	0
1000	00	00	00

Thus $(1000)^3$ = 1000000000. Here R = 4 and Q=2, therefore we have taken two digits from right side of column-4, column-3, column-2 respectively. Since here we have to take two digits from the right side and in last three columns we have only one digit, so we can write 0=00, as it is necessary to follow the rule according to the method discussed earlier.

Ecercise-5

1. Find the cube of the numbers 95, 88, 66, 96, 79.
2. Find the Cube of the numbers 543, 867, 687, 758.
3. Find the cube of the numbers 497546, 64866.
4. Can we make some another rule to find the cube of any positive number?
5. Can we extend this method for negative numbers also?
6. Can we apply the working rules for a fraction also?
7. Can we find the cube of an irrational number using the above method?

6. Biquadratic of a Number

To find the fourth power or biquadratic of any positive integer of any number of digits, we break the given number into two parts A starting from the left side digit and B the remaining digits of the given number using the procedures discussed earlier (Yadav, 2007, 2008, 2018). Thereafter we proceed as follows:

1. Make 5 columns and write the 5 terms of right hand side of the binomial theorem for positive integral index

$$(A+B)^4 = {}^4C_0 A^4 + {}^4C_1 A^3 B^1 + {}^4C_2 A^2 B^2 + {}^4C_3 A^1 B^3 + {}^4C_4 B^4$$

as follows:

Column -1	*Column* -2	*Column* -3	*Column* -4	*Column* -5
A^4	$4 \times A^3 \times B$	$6 \times A^2 \times B^2$	$4 \times A \times B^3$	B^4

2. Evaluate each column separately.
3. Divide the number of digits R of the given number by 2 and find the quotient Q. Q may also be found as: If R = 2m+1 or 2m, where m is a positive integer, then Q = m.
4. Now to find the required result we combine all five parts as:
i. Take as many digits as the quotient value is from the right side of column-5 (let it be P_5) and add the remaining digits (number) in its left side in column–4.

ii. Again take as many digits as the quotient value is from the right side of the column–4 (let it be P_4) and write it in the left side of P_5 (like P_4 P_5) and add the remaining digits (number) in its left side in column-3.

iii. Repeat (i) and (ii) up to column-2 till P_2 and finally find the number P_1 in column-1 after adding remaining digits (numbers) of column–2 and write P_1 to the left of P_2.

Thus we find the required 4th power of the given positive integer as $P_1 P_2 P_3 . P_4 P_5$.

Let us see the method working on some examples:

Example 1: Find the fourth power of 12.

Since the given number is of two digits, therefore R = 2, A = 1, B = 2. Now we make the five columns as follows:

$Column-1$	$Column-2$	$Column-3$	$Column-4$	$Column-5$
A^4	$4 \times A^3 \times B$	$6 \times A^2 \times B^2$	$4 \times A \times B^3$	B^4
$1^4 = 1$	$4 \times 1^3 \times 2 = 8$	$6 \times 1^2 \times 2^2 = 24$	$4 \times 1 \times 2^3 = 32$	$2^4 = 16$
$+1$	$+2$	$+3$	$+1$	16
2	10	27	33	6

Thus $12^4 = 20736$. Here R = 2 and Q = 1, therefore we have taken one digit from right side.

Example 2: Find the fourth power of 111.

Here the given number is of three digits, therefore R = 3, A = 11, B = 1. Now we make the five columns as follows:

Column-1	Column-2	Column-3	Column-4	Column-5
A^4	$4.A^3.B$	$6.A^2.B^2$	$4.A.B^3$	B^4
$11^4=14641$	$4.11^3.1=5324$	$6.11^2.1^2=726$	$4.11.1^3=44$	$1^4=1$
+539	+73	+4 = 730	4	1
=	=			
15180	5397			
15180	7	0	4	1

Thus $111^4 = 151807041$. Here R = 3 and Q = 1, therefore we have taken one digit from right side.

Example 3: Find the fourth power of 1111.

Here the given number is of four digits, therefore R = 4, A = 11, B = 11. Now we make the five columns as follows:

Column-1	Column-2	Column-3	Column-4	Column-5
A^4	$4.A^3.B$	$6.A^2.B^2$	$4.A.B^3$	B^4
$11^4=14641$	$4.11^3.11=$ 58564	$6.11^2.11^2=87846$	$4.11.11^3=$ 58564	$11^4=14641$
+594	+884	+587	+146	41
=	=	= 88433	=	
15235	59448		58710	
15235	48	33	10	41

Thus $(1111)^4 = 1523548331041$. Here R = 4 and Q = 2, therefore we have taken two digits from right side.

Example 4: Find the fourth power of 1302.

Here R = 4, A = 13, B = 02. We make the five columns as:

Column-1	Column-2	Column-3	Column-4	Column-5
A^4	$4.A^3.B$	$6.A^2.B^2$	$4.A.B^3$	B^4
$13^4=28561$	$4.13^3.02=$ 17576	$6.13^2.02^2=4056$	$4.13.02^3=$ 416	$02^4=16$
$+176$	$+40$	$+4$	$+0$	16
=	=	=	=	
28737	17616	4060	416	
28737	16	60	16	16

Thus $(1302)^4 = 2873716601616$. Here R = 4 and Q = 2. Therefore we have taken two digits from the right side of column-5, column-4, column-3, column-2 respectively.

Exercise-6

1. Find the fourth power of the numbers 95, 88, 66, 96, 79.
2. Find the fourth power of the numbers 543, 867, 687, 758.
3. Find the fourth power of the numbers 497546, 64866.
4. Can we make some another rule to find the fourth power of any positive number?
5. Can we extend this method for negative numbers also?
6. Can we apply the working rules for a fraction also?
7. Can we find the fourth power of an irrational number using the above method?

7. Quantic of a Number

To find the fifth power or quantic of any positive integer of any number of digits, we break the given number into two parts A starting from the left side digit and B the remaining digits of the given number using the procedures discussed earlier (Yadav, 2007, 2008, 2018). Thereafter we proceed as follows:

1. Make 6 columns and write the 6 terms of right hand side of the binomial theorem for positive integral index

$$(A+B)^5 = {}^5C_0 A^5 + {}^5C_1 A^4 B^1 + {}^5C_2 A^3 B^2 + {}^5C_3 A^2 B^3 + {}^5C_4 A^1 B^4 + {}^5C_5 B^5$$

as follows:

Column-1	Column-2	Column-3	Column-4	Column-5	Column-6
A^5	$5.A^4.B$	$10.A^3.B^2$	$10.A^2.B^3$	$5.A.B^4$	B^5

2. Evaluate each column separately.
3. Divide the number of digits R of the given number by 2 and find the quotient Q. Q may also be found as: If R = 2m+1 or 2m, where m is a positive integer, then Q = m.
4. Now to find the required result we combine all six parts as:
    i. Take as many digits as the quotient value is from the right side of column-6 (let it be P_6) and add the remaining digits (number) in its left side in column–5.

ii.　Again take as many digits as the quotient value is from the right side of the column–5 (let it be P_5) and write it in the left side of P_6 (like P_5 P_6) and add the remaining digits (number) in its left side in column-4.

iii.　Repeat (i) and (ii) up to column-2 till P_2 and finally find the number P_1 in column-1 after adding remaining digits (numbers) of column–2 and write P_1 to the left of P_2.

Thus we find the required 5th power of the given positive integer as $P_1 P_2 P_3 P_4 P_5 P_6$.

Example 1: Find the fifth power of 23.

Since the given number is of two digits therefore R = 2, A = 2, B = 3. We have six columns:

Column-1	Column-2	Column-3	Column-4	Column-5	Column-6
A^5	$5.A^4.B$	$10.A^3.B^2$	$10.A^2.B^3$	$5.A.B^4$	B^5
2^5	$5.2^4.3$	$10.2^3.3^2$	$10.2^2.3^3$	$5.2.3^4$	3^5
=32	=240	=720	=1080	=810	=243
+32	+83	+116	+83	+24	3
=64	=323	=836	=1163	=834	
64	3	6	3	4	3

Thus $(23)^5 = 6436343$, since Q=1, we took 1 digit from right side.

Exercise-7

1.　Find the fifth power of the numbers 65, 78, 76, 687, 758.

8. Sixth Power of a Number

To find the sixth power of any positive integer of any number of digits, we break the given number into two parts A starting from the left side digit and B the remaining digits of the given number using the method discussed earlier (Yadav, 2007, 2008, 2018). Thereafter we proceed as follows:

1. Make 7 columns and write the 7 terms of right hand side of the binomial theorem for positive integral index

$$(A + B)^6 = A^6 + 6A^5B + 15A^4B^2 + 20A^3B^3 + 15A^2B^4 + 6AB^5 + B^6$$

as follows:

Column-1	Column-2	Column-3	Column-4	Column-5	Column-6	Column-7
A^6	$6.A^5.B$	$15.A^4.B^2$	$20.A^3.B^3$	$15.A^2.B^4$	$5.A.B^5$	B^6

2. Evaluate each column separately.

3. Divide the number of digits R of the given number by 2 and find the quotient Q. Q may also be found as: If R = 2m+1 or 2m, where m is a positive integer, then Q = m.

4. Now to find the required result we combine all seven parts as:

i. Take as many digits as the quotient value is from the right side of column-7 (let it be P_7) and add the remaining digits (number) in its left side in column–6.

ii. Again take as many digits as the quotient value is from the right side of the column–6 (let it be P_6) and write it in the left side of P_7 (like P_6 P_7) and add the remaining digits (number) in its left side in column-5.

iii. Repeat (i) and (ii) up to column-2 till P_2 and finally find the number P_1 in column-1 after adding remaining digits (numbers) of column–2 and write P_1 to the left of P_2.

Thus we find the required 6th power of the given positive integer as P_1 P_2 P_3 P_4 P_5 P_6 P_7.

Example 1: Find the 6th power of 21.

Since the given number is of two digits therefore R = 2, A = 2, B = 1. Here we have to make seven columns:

Column-1	Column-2	Column-3	Column-4	Column-5	Column-6	Column-7
A^6	$6.A^5.B$	$15.A^4.B^2$	$20.A^3.B^3$	$15.A^2.B^4$	$5.A.B^5$	B^6
2^6	$6.2^5.1$	$15.2^4.1^2$	$20.2^3.1^3$	$15.2^2.1^4$	$5.2.1^5$	1^6
=64	=192	=240	=160	=60	=12	=1
+21	+25	+16	+6	+1		
=85	=217	=256	=166	=61		
85	7	6	6	1	2	1

Thus 21^6 = 85766121. Here R = 2, Q = 1, therefore we have taken one digit from the right side of each column up to column-2.

Exercise-8

1. Find the sixth power of the numbers 35, 68, 56, 683, 756.

2. Can we make some another rule to find the sixth power of any positive number?

9. nth Power of a Number

To find the nth power of any positive integer of any number of digits, we break the given number into two parts A starting from the left side digit and B the remaining digits of the given number. For this we first find the number of digits (let it be R) in the given number whose nth power is to be found (Yadav, 2007, 2008, 2018). There may be two cases:

Case I: When the number of digits (R) is odd (let 2m +1), then part A has (m+1) digits from the left side and part B will have the remaining 'm' digits.

Case II: When the number of digits (R) is even (let 2m), then part A has 'm' digits from the left side and part B will have the remaining 'm' digits. In this case both parts A and B have the same number of digits.

It should be kept in mind that in finding A and B, there must not be any change in the order of digits of the given number.

Now we proceed as follows:

1. Make (n+1) columns and write the (n+1) terms of right hand side of the binomial theorem for positive integral index

$$(a + b)^n = C(n, 0)a^n + C(n, 1)a^{n-1}b + C(n, 2)a^{n-2}b^2 + \cdots$$
$$+ C(n, n - 1)ab^{n-1} + C(n, n)b^n$$

where, $C(n, r) = {}^nC_r = \dfrac{n!}{(n-r)!\,r!}$ and $0 \leq r \leq n$, as follows:

Column-1	Column-2	Column-3	..	Column-(n-1)	Column-(n)
$C(n,0)a^n$	$C(n,1)a^{n-1}b$	$C(n,1)a^{n-1}b$	..	$C(n,n-1)ab^{n-1}$	$C(n,n)b^n$

We must not change the order of the columns to avoid the wrong result.

2. Evaluate each column separately.

3. Divide the number of digits R of the given number by 2 and find the quotient Q. Q may also be found as: If R = 2m+1 or 2m, where m is a positive integer, then Q = m.

4. Now to find the required result we combine all n+1 parts as:

i. Take as many digits as the quotient value is from the right side of column-(n+1) (let it be P_{n+1}) and add the remaining digits (number) in its left side in column–n.

ii. Again take as many digits as the quotient value is from the right side of the column–n (let it be P_n) and write it in the left side of P_{n+1} (like $P_n\,P_{n+1}$) and add the remaining digits (number) in its left side in column-(n-1).

iii. Repeat (i) and (ii) up to column-2 till P_2 and finally find the number P_1 in column-1 after adding remaining digits (number) of column–2 and write P_1 to the left of P_2.

Thus we find the required nth power of the given positive integer as

$$P_1 P_2 P_3 ..... P_r .... P_n P_{n+1} \; .$$

Here between any two P_i, (where i = 1, 2, ..., n+1), there is no operation like multiplication. It is just representation of numbers only. Here all P_2 , $P_3,$............., P_{n+1} are numbers of m digits, where m is equal to the quotient Q.

From this method we can develop methods for different exponent values of n one by one as have been previously discussed.

TO FIND THE Nth POWER OF A NEGATIVE INTEGER

To find the nth power of negative integers, we use the fact $(-k)^n = (-1)^n .(k)^n$, where k is any positive integer. Now we find $(k)^n$ as the method discussed before and multiply it by +1 or −1 according to $(-1)^n$ when 'n' is even or odd. Thus we get the result (Yadav, 2007, 2008, 2018).

Example 1: Find the nth power of (-21) if n=6.
Since we can write $(-21)^6 = (-1)^6 (21)^6$.
But $21^6 = 85766121$ and $(-1)^6 = 1$.
Therefore $(-21)^6 = 85766121$

Example 2: Find the nth power of (-12) if n=3.
Since we can write $(-12)^3 = (-1)^3 12^3$.
But $12^3 = 1728$ and $(-1)^3 = -1$.
Therefore $(-12)^3 = -1728$

TO FIND THE Nth POWER OF A RATIONAL NUMBER

Let the given rational number $\dfrac{P}{Q}$ be of terminating form and in terminating decimal form it is represented by

$$\frac{P}{Q} = a_1 a_2 a_3 \ldots\ldots a_i . b_1 b_2 b_3 \ldots\ldots b_r$$

where '.' between a_i and b_1 is a decimal point.

To find the nth power of $\dfrac{P}{Q}$, we proceed as follows:

1. Find the nth power of $(a_1 a_2 a_3 \ldots\ldots a_i b_1 b_2 b_3 \ldots\ldots b_r)$ according to the method discussed above without considering the decimal point between a_i and b_1.

2. Now put the decimal point in the result (1) before (n.r) digits from the right side.

3. If the given rational number is negative, take positive or negative sign according to 'n' is even or odd respectively.

Thus we get the required result (Yadav, 2007, 2008, 2018).

Example 3: Find the nth power of $\dfrac{155}{4}$ if n=3.

Since we have $\dfrac{155}{4} = 38.75$

Therefore to find the cube of it, we first find the cube of 3875 without considering the decimal point. Here we have R = 4, A = 38, B = 75.

Now we make the table of four columns as follows:

Column-1	Column-2	Column-3	Column-4
A^3	$3.A^2.B.$	$3.A.B^2$	B^3
$38^3=54872$	$3.38^2.75=324900$	$3.38.75^2=641250$	$75^3=421875$
$+3313$	$+6454$	$+4218$	75
$=58185$	$=331354$	$=645468$	
58185	54	68	75

Thus $3875^3 = 58185546875$. Since here n = 3, r = 2, therefore n.r = 3.2 = 6. Hence we put decimal point before six digits from the right side. Therefore $\left(\dfrac{155}{4}\right)^3 = (38.75)^3 = 58185.546875$

Note: This method is also applicable for n = 1. But in this case no extra operation is required (Yadav, 2007, 2008, 2018).

Applications

If we know the nth power of 0, 1, 2, 3, 4, 5, 6, 7, 8, 9 and have simple knowledge of multiplication then we can find the nth power of any integer or rational numbers in terminating decimal form by Anurupyena Binomial Method (Yadav, 2007, 2008, 2018).

Limitations of Anurupyena Binomial Method

This method is not applicable for finding the nth power of irrational numbers and rational numbers (in non-terminating decimal forms) (Yadav, 2007, 2008, 2018).

References

Halai, C. (2018). Vedic Mathematics Inside Out, The Write Place, Pune, IX-X, 111-113, 117-119, 221-225.

Knnojiya, D. S. & Yadav, D. K. (2008). Algorithm of Annuruppen – Binomial Method, International Journal of math and sci and Engg. Appls (IJMSEA), 2(4), 101-112.

Maharaja S. B. K. T. (2015). Vedic Mathematics, Motilal Banarsi Dass Publishers Pvt Ltd, 17-22, Delhi, India.

Sharma, A., Sharma, A. K. (2024). Significant Contribution of Ancient Bhartiya Mathematics towards Vasudhaiva Kutumbakam, The International Journal of Bharatiya Knowledge System, 1, 121-133.

Shashtri, P. R. (2011) Vedic Mathematics Made Easy, Arihant Publication (I) Pvt. Ltd. Meerut (UP), 50-53, 56-57.

Shashtri, P. R. (2011). Vedic Mathematics Made Easy, Arihant Publications (I), Meerut, 50-53.

Thakur, R. (2019). Advance Vedic Mathematics, Rupa Publication India Pvt. Ltd, New Delhi, 19-22, 34-47.

Yadav, D. K. (2007), Aanuruppen Binomial Method to find the nth power of integers and rational numbers in terminating decimal forms, Acta Ciencia Indica, Mathematics, 33 (M) (2), 647-655.

Yadav, D. K. (2018). Academic Paper: Anurupyena Binomial Method: An Application of Binomial Method in Vedic Mathematics, Grin Verlag, Germany, 1-22.

Books By Author

1. A Study of Indefinite Nonintegrable Functions, GRIN Verlag Publishing, Germany, ISBN: 9783668312791

2. Six Conjectures on Integration: Extension of Nonelementary Functions, GRIN Verlag Publishing, Germany, ISBN: 9783668357990

3. Dominating Sequential Functions: Superset of Elementary Functions, GRIN Verlag Publishing, Germany, ISBN: 9783668464001

4. Multi-dimensional Arithmetic Progression, GRIN Verlag Publishing, Germany, ISBN: 9783346135766

5. Multi-dimensional Geometric Progression, GRIN Verlag Publishing, Germany, ISBN: 9783346174161

6. Nonelementary Integrals, Notion Press, India, ISBN: 9798890674852

7. Jivan ki Kavita, Notion Press, India, ISBN: 9798887178165, 2022.

8. Bunch of Poems, Notion Press, India, ISBN: 9798887335049, 2022.

9. Kalpanik Kavita, Notion Press, India, ISBN: 9798889516316, 2023.

10. Srishti Leela, Notion Press, India, ISBN: 9798890027467, 2023.

11. Kabutarbaj, Notion Press, India, ISBN: 9798893221497, 2024.

12. Impact of Science & Technology on Society, Vayu Education of India, Delhi, 2009

Suggestion Box

52

Suggestions will be welcomed through email id

mdrdkyadav@gmail.com